MathFlare

Name: _______________________

Class: _________

Teacher: _______________________

Introduction

As parents and educators, we recognize the pivotal role mathematics plays in shaping a child's academic journey and future success. Yet, the path to mathematical proficiency can often seem daunting, fraught with challenges and complexities. That's where the transformative power of MathFlare Workbooks shine through, illuminating the way forward with clarity, precision, and purpose.

Introducing MathFlare Workbooks – a beacon of guidance, a testament to excellence, and a catalyst for achievement. Crafted with meticulous care and expertise, MathFlare Workbooks stand as paragons of educational excellence, designed to nurture young minds, ignite a passion for learning, and develop a deep-rooted understanding of mathematical concepts.

Picture this: your child eagerly delves into the pages of Mathflare Workbook, greeted by a step-by-step guide illuminated with vivid examples that demystify complex mathematical concepts. With each turn of the page, they embark on a journey of discovery, encountering thoughtfully curated practice questions that reinforce learning and hone problem-solving skills. And when they unveil the answers to those very questions, a sense of accomplishment blossoms within them – a tangible reward for their hard work and dedication.

But MathFlare Workbooks are more than just tools for learning; they are pathways to comprehension, fostering a deep-seated understanding of mathematical concepts through a sequential, logical flow. From fundamental principles to advanced problem-solving strategies, every chapter builds upon the last, ensuring a robust foundation upon which future knowledge can be constructed.

As parents, we yearn for nothing more than to see our children thrive, to witness the spark of inspiration ignited within them as they conquer academic challenges with confidence and poise. MathFlare Workbooks serve as partners in this noble endeavor, offering not just practice questions, but the keys to unlocking a world of opportunity.

And for teachers, MathFlare Workbooks stand as invaluable allies in the quest to cultivate mathematical proficiency in the classroom. With answers readily available, instructors can focus on guiding and nurturing their students, confident in the knowledge that MathFlare Workbooks provide a solid framework upon which to build.

In the pages of MathFlare Workbooks, we find not just the promise of academic excellence, but the seeds of a brighter tomorrow. So let us embrace the power of mathematics, let us champion the journey of learning, and let us pave the way for a generation of young minds poised to shape the world. With MathFlare Workbooks as our guide, the possibilities are infinite, and the future, bright.

Table of Contents

MathFlare
MATH
WORKBOOK
Grade 2
Step by Step Guide
and Essential Practice
with Answers
Addition
Subtraction
Multiplication
Place Value and
Expanded
Notations
Geometry
MathFlare Publishing

MathFlare
MATH
WORKBOOK
Grade 2-3
Step by Step Guide
and Essential Practice
with Answers
Addition
Subtraction
Multiplication
and Division
Place Value and
Expanded
Notations
Geometry
MathFlare Publishing

MathFlare
MATH
WORKBOOK
Grade 3
Step by Step Guide
and Essential Practice
with Answers
Multiplication
and Division
Decimals
Place Value and
Expanded
Notations
Fractions
and Geometry
MathFlare Publishing

MathFlare
MATH
WORKBOOK
Grade 1
Step by Step Guide
and Essential Practice
with Answers
Counting and
Numbers
Addition and
Subtraction
Place Value and
Expanded
Notations
Understanding
Time
MathFlare Publishing

MathFlare
MATH
WORKBOOK
Grade 1-2
Step by Step Guide
and Essential Practice
with Answers
Counting and
Numbers
Addition and
Subtraction
Place Value and
Expanded
Notations
Understanding
Time
MathFlare Publishing

MathFlare
MATH
WORKBOOK
Grade 3-4
Step by Step Guide
and Essential Practice
with Answers
Addition
Subtraction
Multiplication
Division
Place Value and
Expanded
Notations
Fractions
and Geometry
MathFlare Publishing

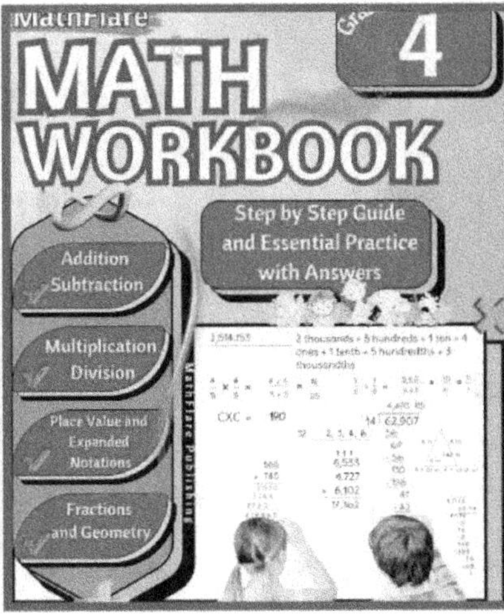
MathFlare
MATH
WORKBOOK
Grade 4
Step by Step Guide
and Essential Practice
with Answers
Addition
Subtraction
Multiplication
Division
Place Value and
Expanded
Notations
Fractions
and Geometry
MathFlare Publishing

MathFlare
MATH
WORKBOOK
Grade 4-5
Step by Step Guide
and Essential Practice
with Answers
Multiplication
Division
Place Value and
Expanded
Notations
Fractions
and Geometry
Unit
Conversion
MathFlare Publishing

MathFlare
Grade 5
MATH
WORKBOOK
Step by Step Guide
and Essential Practice
with Answers
Multiplication
Division
Place Value and
Expanded
Notations
Fractions
and Geometry
Unit
Conversion
MathFlare Publishing

MathFlare
Grade 5-6
MATH
WORKBOOK
Step by Step Guide
and Essential Practice
with Answers
Multiplication
Division
Place Value and
Expanded
Notations
Fractions
and Geometry
Units and
Statistics
MathFlare Publishing

MathFlare
Grade 6
MATH
WORKBOOK
Step by Step Guide
and Essential Practice
with Answers
Integers and
Statistics
Arithmetic and
Pre-Algebra
Fractions
and Geometry
Ratio and
Percentage
MathFlare Publishing

MathFlare
Grade 6-7
MATH
WORKBOOK
Step by Step Guide
and Essential Practice
with Answers
Arithmetic and
Pre-Algebra
Ratio, Percent
Proportion
Geometry
Statistics
MathFlare Publishing

MathFlare
Grade 7
MATH
WORKBOOK
Step by Step Guide
and Essential Practice
with Answers
Pre-Algebra
Ratio, Percent
Proportion
Geometry
Statistics
MathFlare Publishing

MathFlare
Grade 7-8
MATH
WORKBOOK
Step by Step Guide
and Essential Practice
with Answers
Pre-Algebra
Ratio, Percent
Proportion
Geometry and
Cartesian
Plane
Statistics
MathFlare Publishing

MathFlare
Grade 8-9
MATH
WORKBOOK
Step by Step Guide
and Essential Practice
with Answers
Pre-Algebra
Ratio, Proportion
and Percentage
Linear
Equations
Geometry and
Cartesian Plane
MathFlare Publishing

MathFlare
Grade 8
MATH
WORKBOOK
Step by Step Guide
and Essential Practice
with Answers
Pre-Algebra
Percentage
Linear
Equations
Geometry
MathFlare Publishing

Pre-Algebra

Order of Operations (PEMDAS)

The order of operations, often remembered by the acronym PEMDAS, stands for:

- **Parentheses**: Perform operations inside parentheses first.
- **Exponents**: Evaluate exponents (powers and roots) next.
- **Multiplication and Division**: Perform multiplication and division from left to right.
- **Addition and Subtraction**: Perform addition and subtraction from left to right.

The order of operations helps to clarify which operations should be performed first in a mathematical expression to ensure consistent and accurate results.

- **Parentheses**: Evaluate expressions within parentheses first. If there are nested parentheses, start with the innermost ones and work your way out.

    1. Example: $2 \times (3 + 4) = 2 \times 7 = 14$

- **Exponents**: Evaluate expressions with exponents (powers and roots) next.

    1. Example: $2^3 + 4 = 8 + 4 = 12$

- **Multiplication and Division**: Perform multiplication and division from left to right.

    1. Example: $2 \times 3 + 4 = 6 + 4 = 10$

    2. Example: $6 \div 2 \times 3 = 3 \times 3 = 9$

- **Addition and Subtraction**: Perform addition and subtraction from left to right.

    1. Example: $2 + 3 \times 4 = 2 + 12 = 14$

    2. Example: $10 - 4 \div 2 = 10 - 2 = 8$

<u>Solving Equations (One Side)</u>

Solving one-step equations involves performing a single operation to isolate the variable and find its value.

Let's solve an equation step by step: $16 + x = 31$

1. **Identify the Goal**:

    The goal is to isolate the variable x on one side of the equation.

2. **Simplify the Equation**: Combine like terms on both sides of the equation, if necessary.

    The equation is already simplified.

3. **Undo Addition or Subtraction**: If there's addition or subtraction involving the variable, undo it by performing the opposite operation on both sides of the equation.

    Since x is being added to 16, we'll undo this operation by subtracting 16 from both sides of the equation:

    $$16 + x - 16 = 31 - 16$$

4. **Isolate the Variable**: Ensure that the variable is alone on one side of the equation.

    $$x = 15$$

5. **Check Your Solution**: Substitute the value of x back into the original equation to verify that it satisfies the equation.

    $$16 + 15 = 31$$

    $$31 = 31$$

    The equation is balanced.

Solving Inequalities

Inequalities are mathematical expressions that compare the relative sizes of two values. They are used to express relationships where one quantity is:

- "<" (less than),
- ">" (greater than),
- "<=" (less than or equal to),
- ">=" (greater than or equal to),
- and "≠" (not equal to) another quantity.

For example:

$$y + -10 \leq -8$$

To isolate y, we need to get rid of the constant term -10. Since -10 is being subtracted from y, we can undo this operation by adding 10 to both sides of the inequality:

$$y - 10 + 10 \leq -8 + 10$$

$$y \leq 2$$

To check the solution:

$$2 - 10 \leq -8$$

$$-8 = -8$$

The inequality is true when $y = 2$

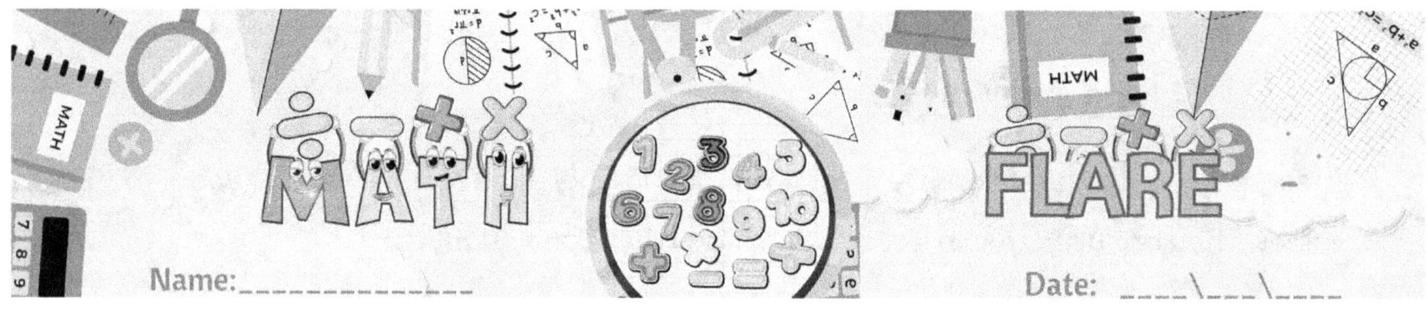

Order of Operations (PEMDAS)
Evaluate Expressions.

1. $(1 + 3)(10 + 7) =$

2. $(5^2) \times (2^2) + 4 =$

3. $4 + 2^2 + 9 + 6^2 =$

4. $7 + 6^2 + 7 + 2^2 =$

5. $(3^2) \times (1^2) + 10 =$

6. $4 \times (8 + 8) =$

7. $7 + 4^2 + 8 + 2^2 =$

8. $10 + 6 - 1 + 7 =$

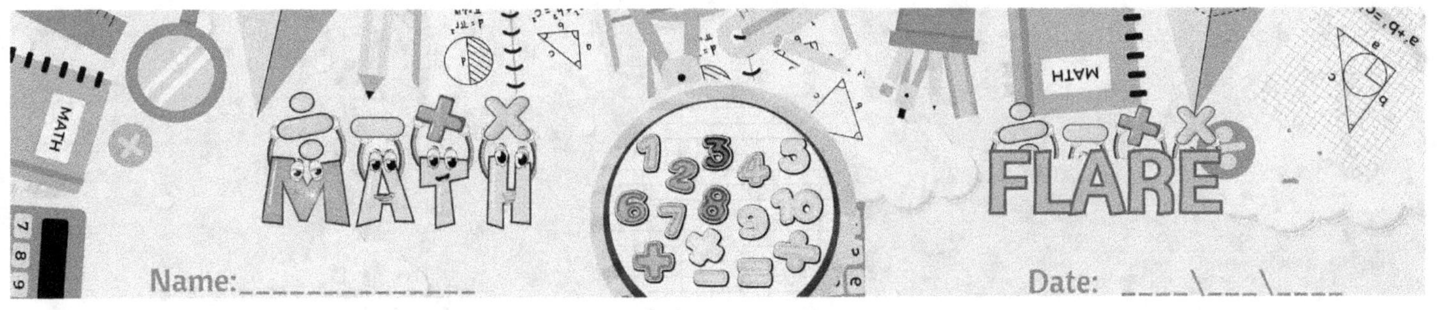

9. $(5 + 7)^2 =$

10. $(5 + 1)^2 =$

11. $1 + 5 + 7 + 3 =$

12. $3(6 + 5) =$

13. $(3 + 7) \times (2 + 6) =$

14. $7 + 10^2 =$

15. $8 \times (9 + 4) =$

16. $(3 + 10)^2 + (2 + 6)^2 =$

17. $(4 + 6) \times (4 + 10) =$

18. $(3 + 5)(5 + 7) =$

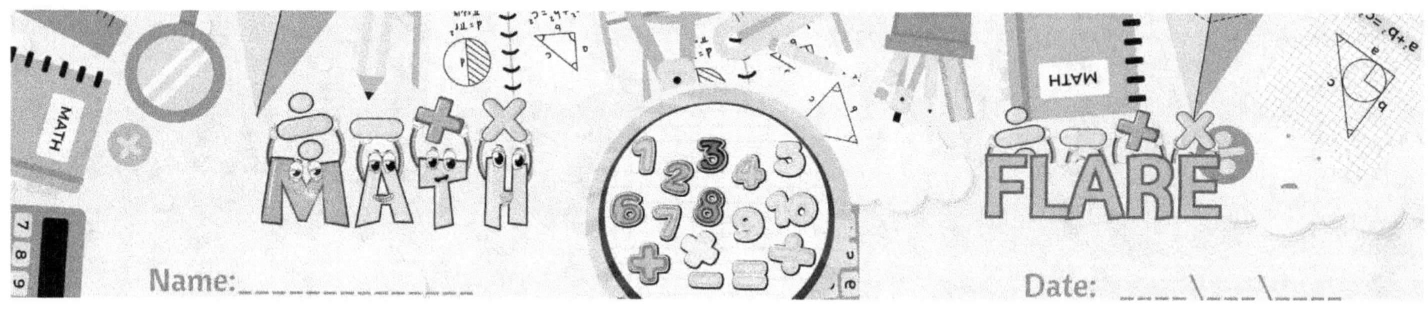

19. $(4 + 8) \div 7 =$

20. $3 + 1^2 + 7 + 5^2 =$

21. $(2 + 6) \div 1 =$

22. $8 \times (5 + 9) =$

23. $(5 + 2)^2 + (5 + 8)^2 =$

24. $1 + 2 + 3 =$

25. $(8 + 7) \div 4 =$

26. $6 + 5^2 =$

27. $(10^2) \times (7^2) + 5 =$

28. $(2 + 7)^2 =$

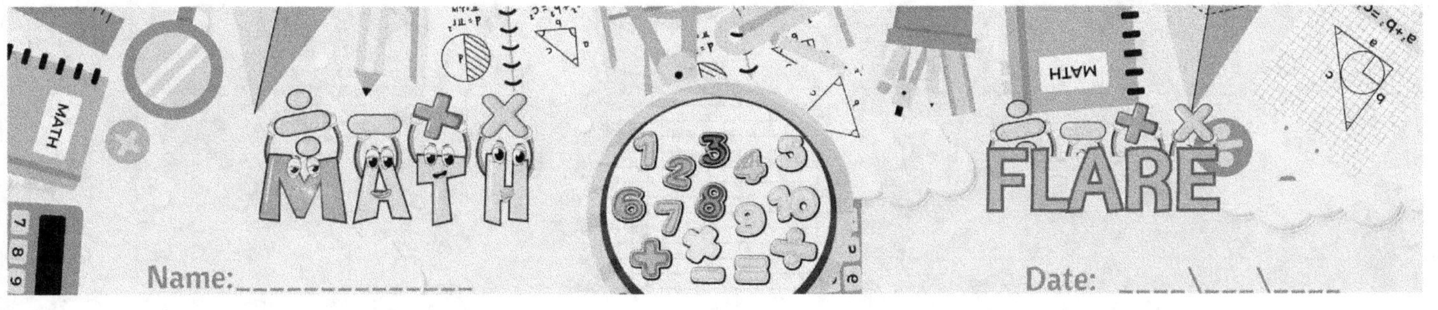

29. $(10 + 9) \times (2 + 9) =$

30. $10 + 10 + 6 =$

31. $(4 + 7)^2 + (4 + 3)^2 =$

32. $7 \times 8 \times 3 =$

33. $2 \times (8 + 8) =$

34. $(9 + 5)(9 + 3) =$

35. $(2^2) \times (3^2) + 3 =$

36. $9 + 7^2 + 4 + 2^2 =$

37. $8(2 + 10) =$

38. $(1 + 1)^2 + (10 + 1)^2 =$

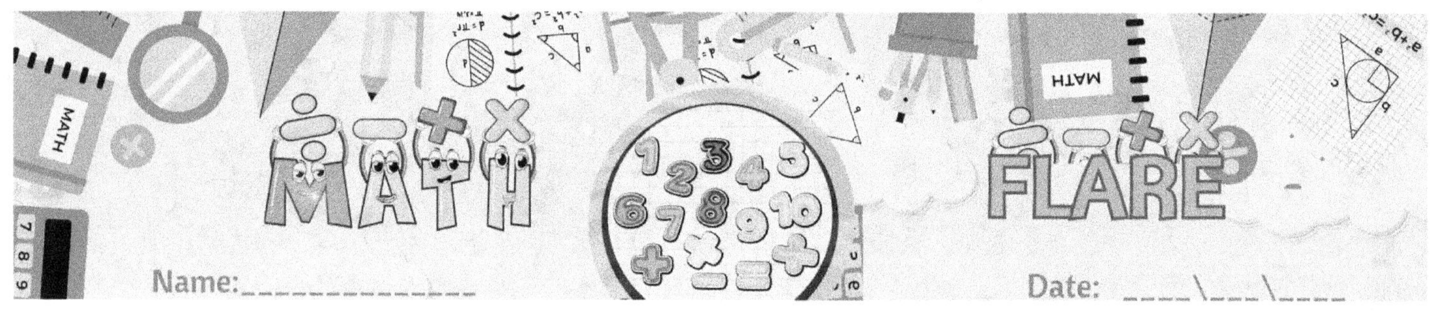

39. $(10 + 3) \div 10 =$

40. $6 + 3^2 =$

41. $(10 + 5)^2 =$

42. $5 \times (9 + 10) =$

43. $(1 + 9) \div 2 =$

44. $(4 + 8) \times (2 + 9) =$

45. $(1^2) \times (3^2) + 5 =$

46. $8 \times 6 =$

47. $(10 \times 10) - (4 + 6) =$

48. $(4 + 7)^2 =$

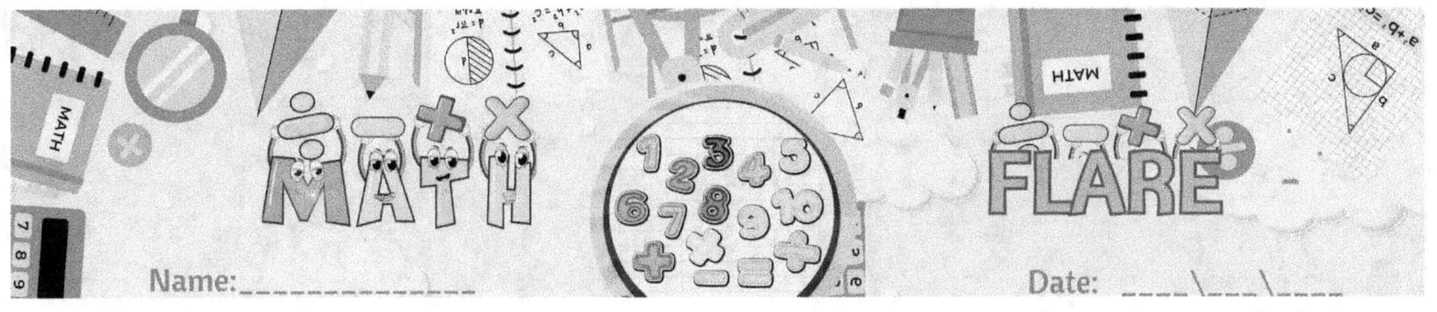

49. $5 \times (4 + 3) =$

50. $6 + 9 + 2 =$

51. $(3 \times 5) - (8 + 3) =$

52. $(2 + 9)(9 + 8) =$

53. $4 + 3 + 9 =$

54. $(8 + 3) \times (8 + 1) =$

55. $10 + 1 + 1 =$

56. $9 + 5^2 + 3 + 4^2 =$

57. $4 + 10 - 2 + 7 =$

58. $7 + 8^2 =$

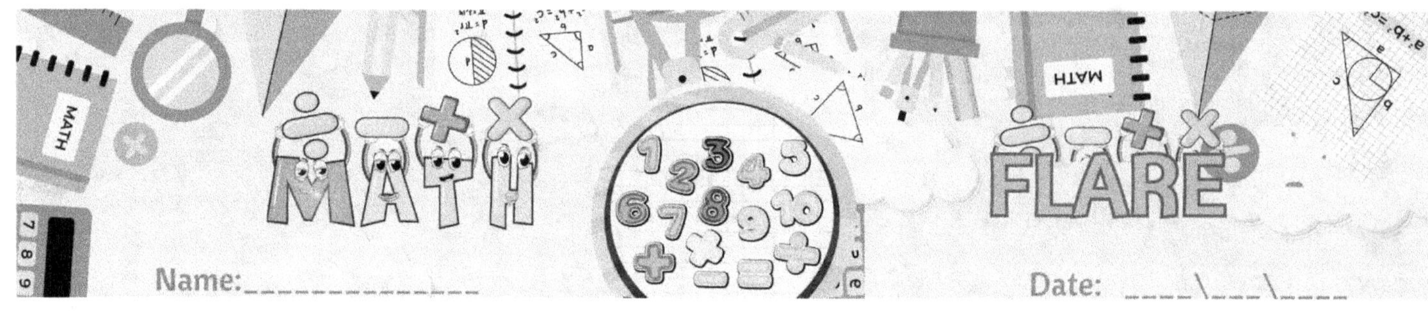

59. $10 \times 6 + 8 =$

60. $6 \times (10 \div 10) =$

61. $(2 \times 3) - (5 + 6) =$

62. $9 + 4 + 7 =$

63. $(1^2) \times (3^2) + 7 =$

64. $(2 \times 6) - (4 + 6) =$

65. $(7^2) \times (6^2) + 3 =$

66. $2 \times (8 + 5) =$

67. $10 + 9^2 + 1 + 8^2 =$

68. $(2 + 5) \div 3 =$

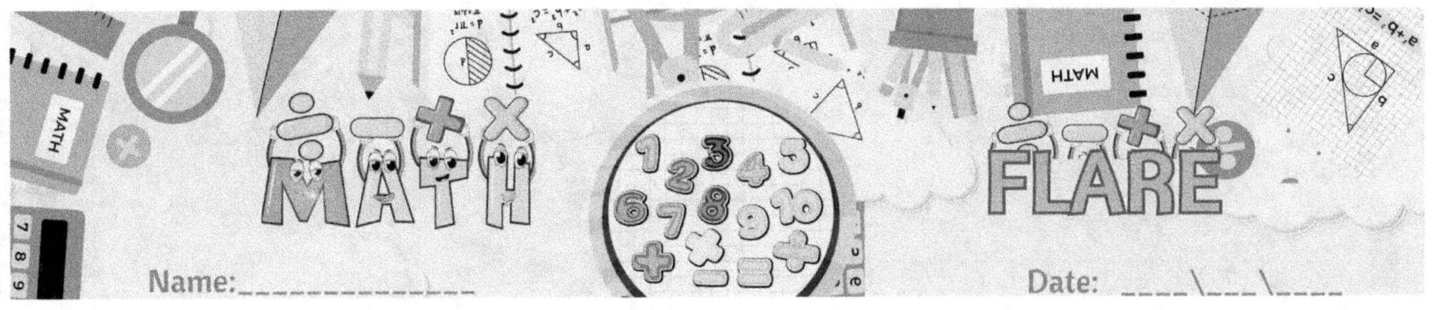

69. $1 + 9^2 + 9 + 5^2 =$

70. $(3 + 8)^2 =$

71. $(3 + 7)^2 + (8 + 5)^2 =$

72. $6 + 2^2 + 5 + 9^2 =$

73. $3 + 2^2 =$

74. $(8^2) \times (9^2) + 7 =$

75. $4 + 1 + 2 =$

76. $5 + 4 + 6 =$

77. $(8^2) \times (6^2) + 1 =$

78. $(3 + 2) \times (7 + 5) =$

79. $(4 + 1) \times (6 + 3) =$

80. $(4 + 2)(9 + 8) =$

81. $1 + 10 + 9 =$

82. $1 \times 8 + 1 =$

83. $4 \times (6 + 7) =$

84. $8 \times (4 + 10) =$

85. $5 + 2^2 + 3 + 9^2 =$

86. $(4^2) \times (6^2) + 9 =$

87. $(6 + 3)^2 + (3 + 4)^2 =$

88. $6(9 + 1) =$

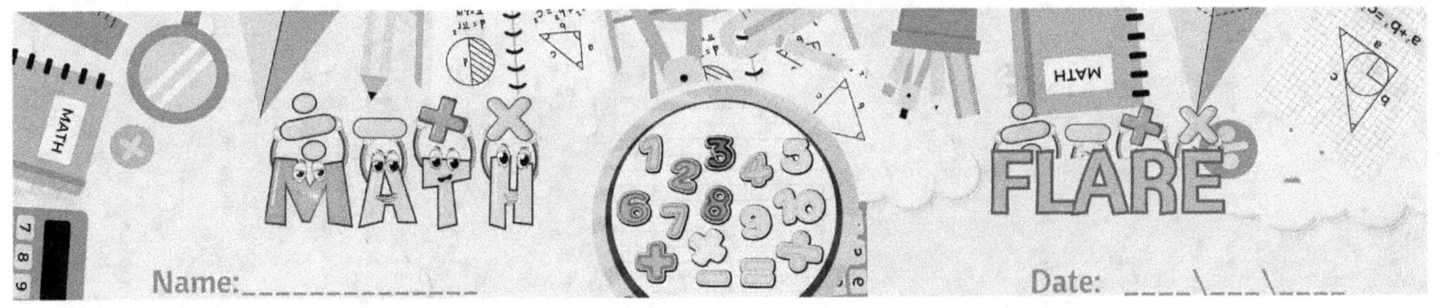

89. $(9 + 4)(3 + 1) =$

90. $8 \times 6 + 10 =$

91. $9 \times 4 =$

92. $(1 \times 4) - (4 + 6) =$

93. $(6 \times 5) - (1 + 4) =$

94. $6 + 9 + 8 =$

95. $1 + 3 + 9 + 8 =$

96. $9 + 9^2 =$

97. $(4 + 4) \div 6 =$

98. $8(7 + 3) =$

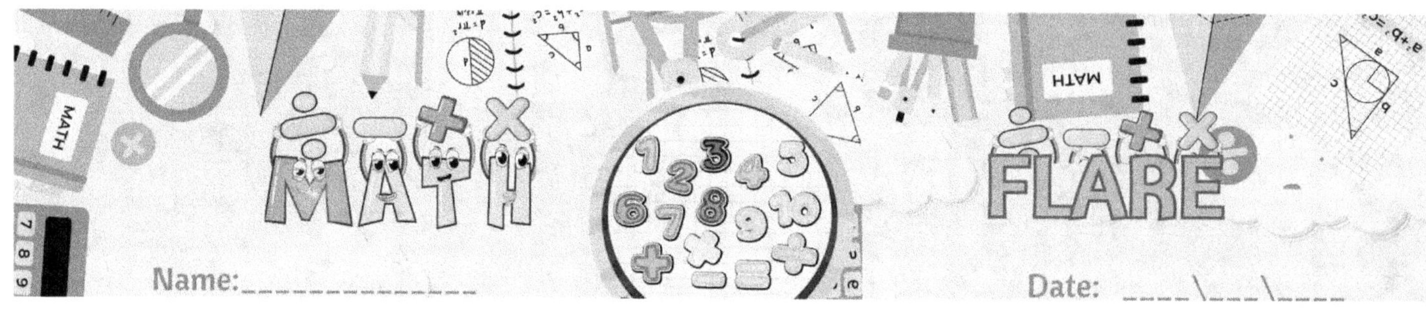

99. $3 \times 8 =$

100. $2 \times 1 =$

101. $(4^2) \times (7^2) + 1 =$

102. $9 + 1 + 7 =$

103. $8(3 + 6) =$

104. $(1 + 10)^2 + (4 + 2)^2 =$

105. $3 \times (10 + 9) =$

106. $(8^2) \times (1^2) + 10 =$

107. $(6 + 6) \div 6 =$

108. $3 \times 9 + 3 =$

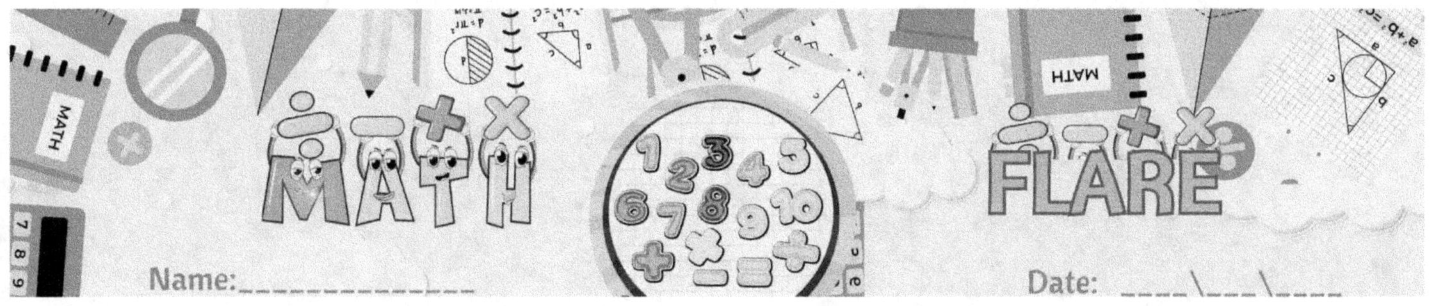

109. $6 \times (4 + 6) =$

110. $(4^2) \times (1^2) + 2 =$

111. $(9^2) \times (4^2) + 5 =$

112. $(7^2) \times (8^2) + 6 =$

113. $10 + 7 - 5 + 5 =$

114. $(6 + 2) \times (8 + 9) =$

115. $10 + 3 + 4 =$

116. $9 \times 9 + 5 =$

117. $(2 + 8)^2 + (7 + 5)^2 =$

118. $8 + 4^2 =$

119. $2 \times 7 \times 5 =$

120. $3 + 3 + 9 + 6 =$

121. $9 + 2^2 =$

122. $(10 + 7)^2 + (6 + 2)^2 =$

123. $4 \times 6 =$

124. $(2 + 10) \div 4 =$

125. $5 + 10 + 3 + 4 =$

126. $10 \times (8 + 6) =$

127. $6 + 1 - 1 + 8 =$

128. $(10 + 10) \div 4 =$

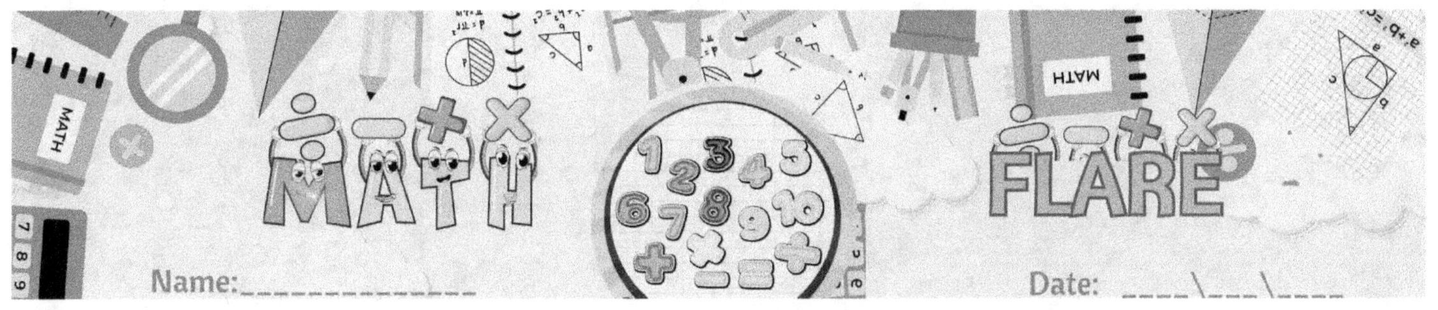

129. $(4 + 4)^2 + (3 + 2)^2 =$

130. $7 \times 10 =$

131. $(8 + 1)^2 + (6 + 9)^2 =$

132. $(7^2) \times (6^2) + 7 =$

133. $(8^2) \times (2^2) + 6 =$

134. $(6^2) \times (5^2) + 9 =$

135. $2 + 5 + 2 =$

136. $4 + 5 + 3 =$

137. $10 \times 9 + 1 =$

138. $(2 + 8)^2 =$

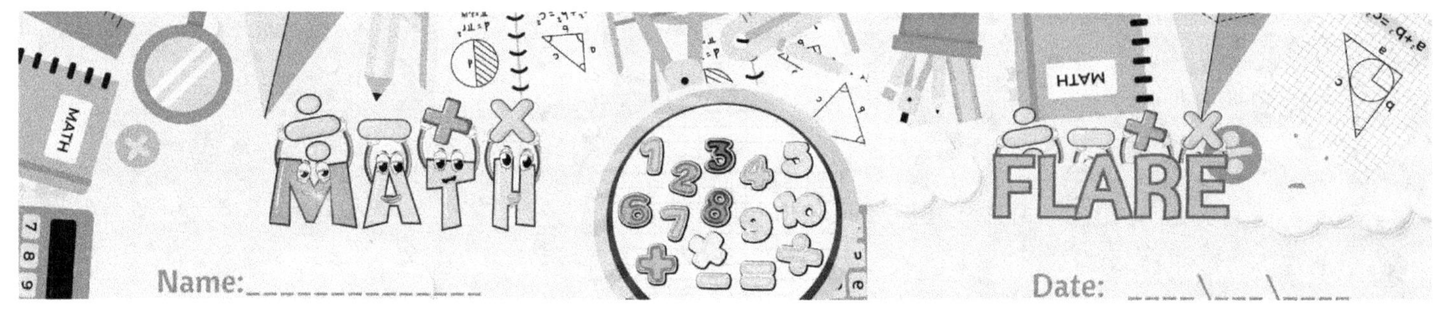

139. $6 + 8 + 10 =$

140. $(5^2) \times (2^2) + 5 =$

141. $(9 \times 3) - (7 + 6) =$

142. $3 \times 2 =$

143. $8 + 2^2 + 2 + 1^2 =$

144. $9 + 3 + 10 =$

145. $(3 \times 4) - (6 + 6) =$

146. $3 + 10^2 + 1 + 9^2 =$

147. $9 \times (5 + 8) =$

148. $1 + 8 + 9 + 8 =$

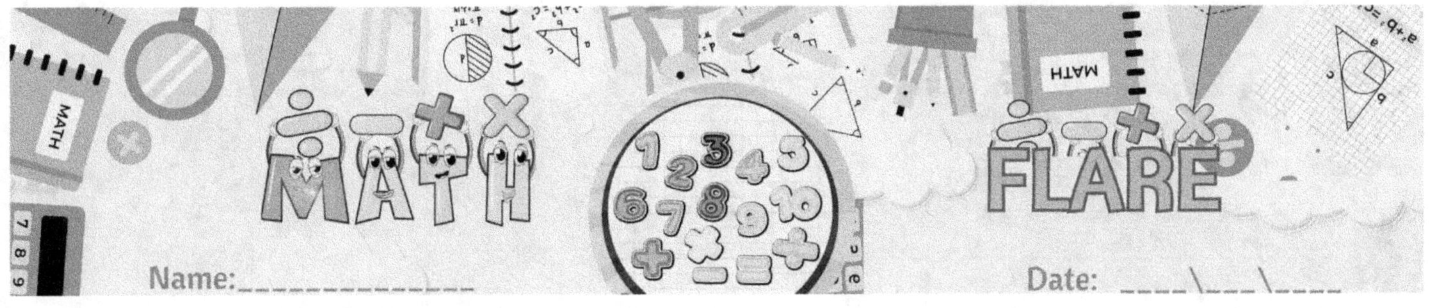

Equations (One Side)
Solve for the variable.

149. $2 + 9m = 164$

150. $y \times 10 = 20$

151. $14 + 3m = 20$

152. $k + 18 = 37$

153. $63 \div k = 7$

154. $x \div 6 = 6$

155. $6m + 1 = 103$

156. $1 + z = 9$

157. $x \div 20 = 19$

158. $x + 4 = 16$

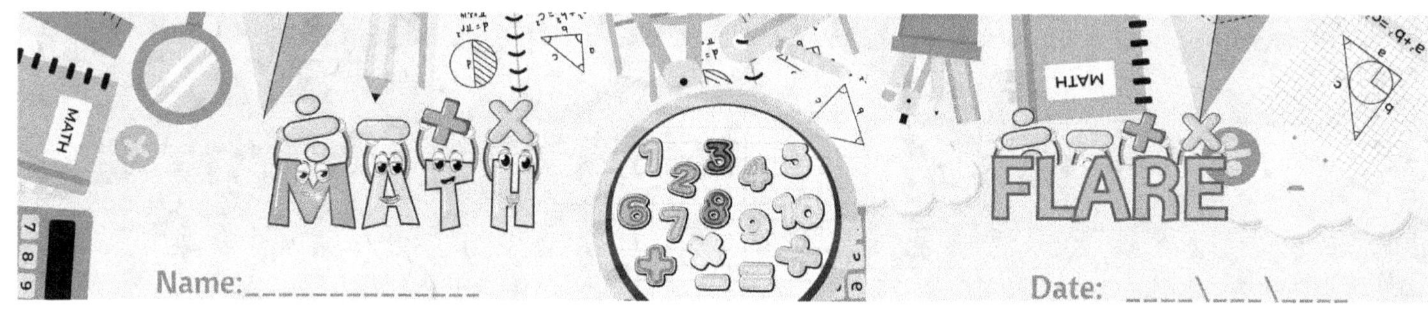

159. $x + 15 = 30$

160. $15 \times y = 15$

161. $z + 11 = 21$

162. $10k - 16 = 124$

163. $k \div 6 = 19$

164. $m - 2 = 18$

165. $29 - 10y = 9$

166. $13 + 8y = 69$

167. $125 - 7z = 6$

168. $14 - x = 8$

169. $11 \times x = 33$

170. $y \times 3 = 18$

171. $k + 5 = 12$

172. $3 \times m = 36$

173. $119 - 14z = 7$

174. $20 \times m = 340$

175. $9z - 10 = 116$

176. $11 - k = 3$

177. $10k + 5 = 145$

178. $19 - k = 3$

179. $x + 15 = 25$

180. $y \div 2 = 20$

181. $2y + 8 = 34$

182. $x - 1 = 5$

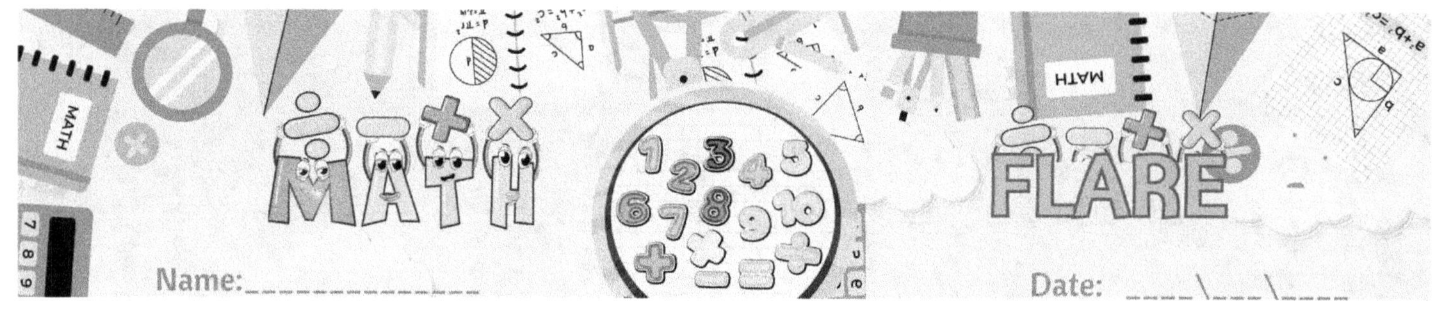

183. $18y - 20 = 142$

184. $x \times 17 = 153$

185. $56 - 4y = 4$

186. $3 \times k = 39$

187. $176 \div k = 16$

188. $13x + 10 = 231$

189. $m \times 2 = 32$

190. $12y - 9 = 39$

191. $17 - z = 13$

192. $18 + 6m = 42$

193. $k \times 17 = 68$

194. $3x - 18 = 36$

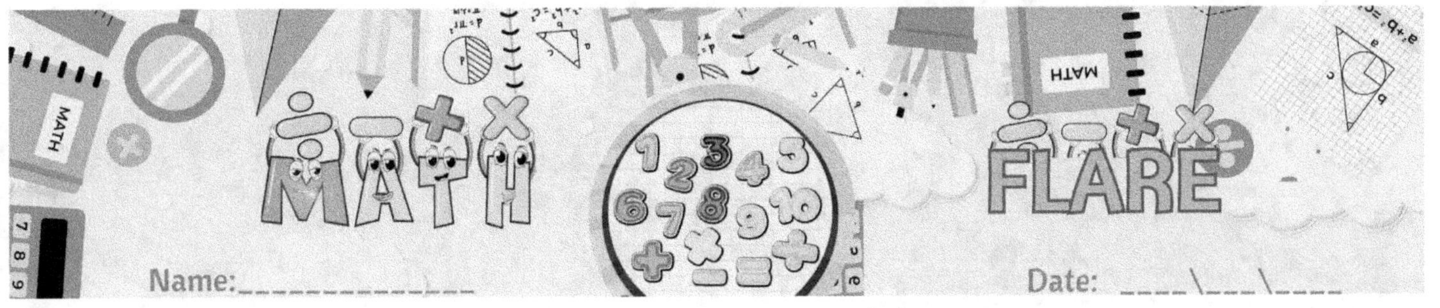

195. $y \times 12 = 240$

196. $k + 16 = 24$

197. $m + 17 = 36$

198. $k + 1 = 6$

199. $75 \div m = 15$

200. $15x + 6 = 126$

201. $56 - 13k = 4$

202. $m - 6 = 11$

203. $2 + 8x = 26$

204. $208 \div y = 13$

205. $x \times 16 = 80$

206. $z - 1 = 7$

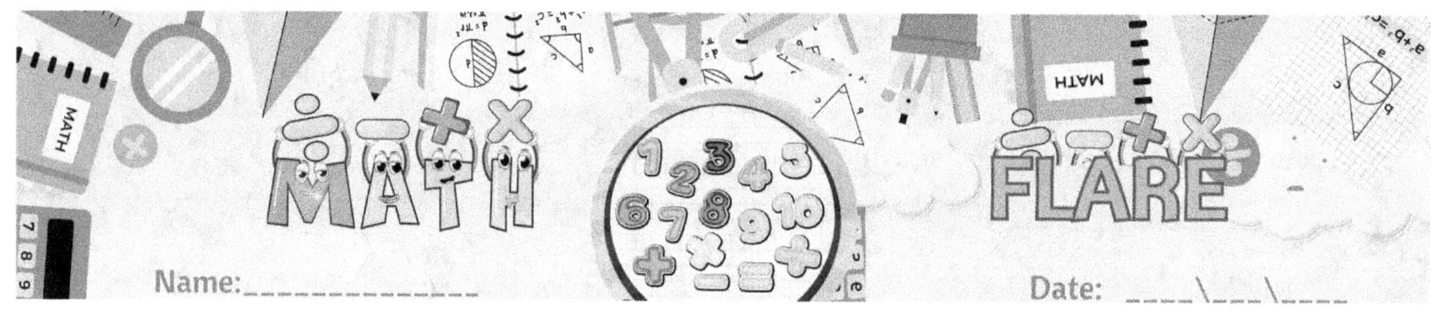

207. $1k + 19 = 24$

208. $12 + 5y = 62$

209. $2 + y = 17$

210. $17 - k = 14$

211. $z - 11 = 6$

212. $19x - 16 = 364$

213. $k \div 10 = 3$

214. $z \div 9 = 11$

215. $17k - 1 = 169$

216. $4m - 12 = 0$

217. $33 - 6x = 9$

218. $y \times 19 = 209$

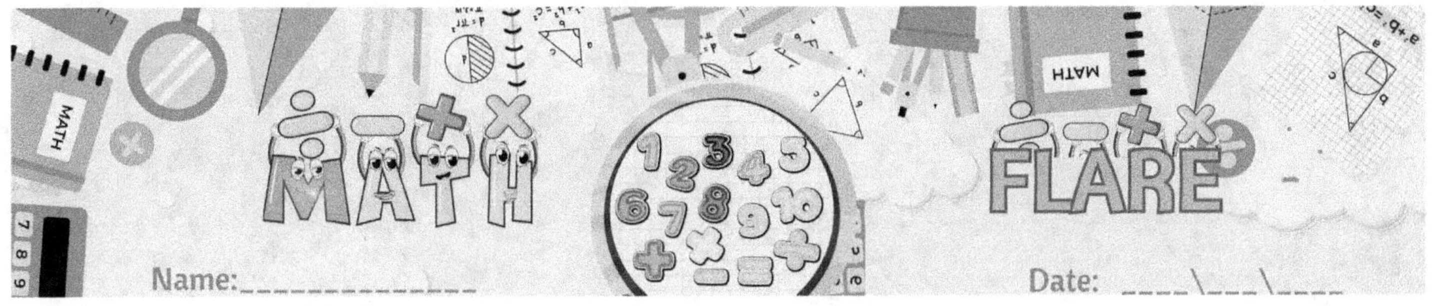

219. $82 - 5x = 2$

220. $x - 7 = 8$

221. $4 + 10x = 104$

222. $m \times 2 = 26$

223. $m \times 3 = 48$

224. $y \div 4 = 3$

225. $1z - 3 = 2$

226. $6z - 19 = 53$

227. $k - 8 = 12$

228. $19x + 6 = 348$

229. $80 - 13x = 2$

230. $19 - y = 7$

231. $z \div 17 = 10$

232. $7 \times z = 77$

233. $7 + 13y = 85$

234. $1 + z = 20$

235. $y \div 17 = 2$

236. $m - 8 = 3$

237. $k \times 11 = 11$

238. $z + 7 = 10$

239. $z - 4 = 4$

240. $8y - 3 = 61$

241. $k \div 13 = 20$

242. $16 + m = 28$

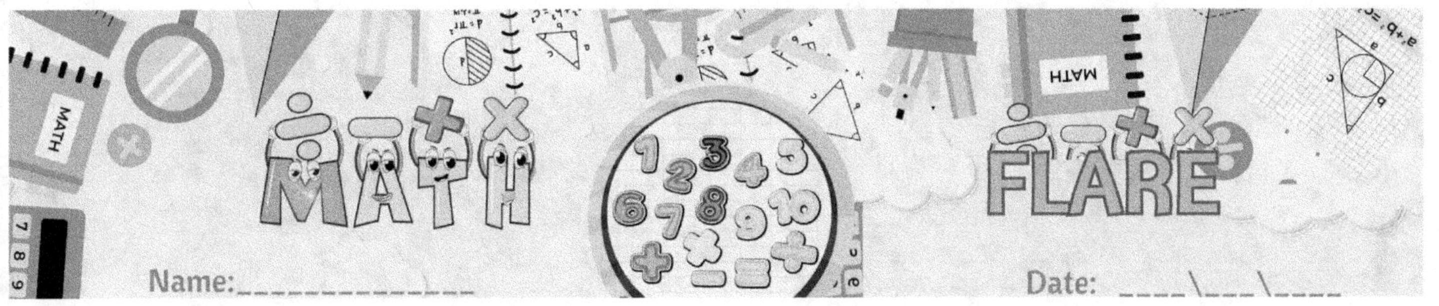

Name:________________   Date: ______________

243. $17 + 8z = 177$

244. $293 - 19k = 8$

245. $z - 9 = 1$

246. $m \times 14 = 182$

247. $10 + 12k = 250$

248. $m - 2 = 9$

249. $3m - 8 = 1$

250. $m - 15 = 2$

251. $16 + 1x = 19$

252. $x - 9 = 0$

253. $10 + 7x = 143$

254. $16 \div z = 2$

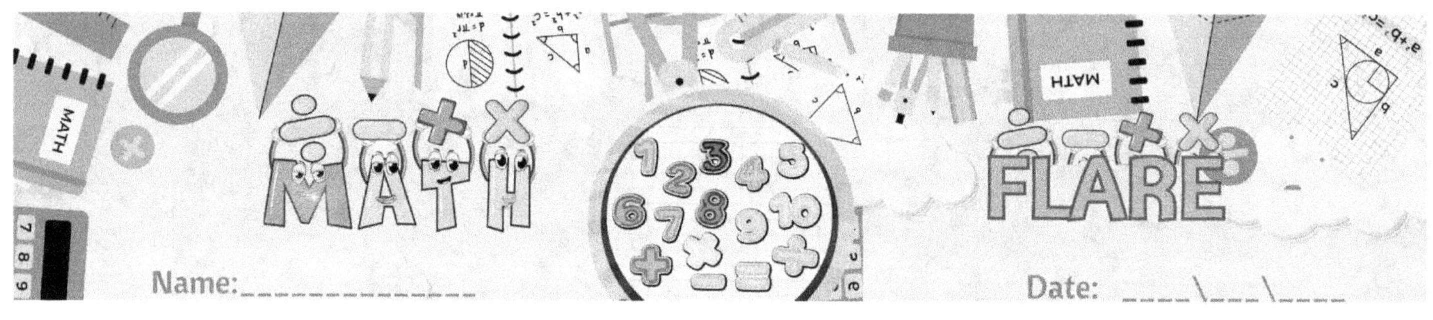

255. $17z + 11 = 130$

256. $9 + 4y = 85$

257. $13 - z = 3$

258. $19y - 17 = 268$

259. $z \div 18 = 11$

260. $11 + 9y = 146$

261. $18 \times z = 162$

262. $x + 13 = 31$

263. $m - 5 = 13$

264. $z - 8 = 2$

265. $9m + 18 = 162$

266. $z \times 9 = 135$

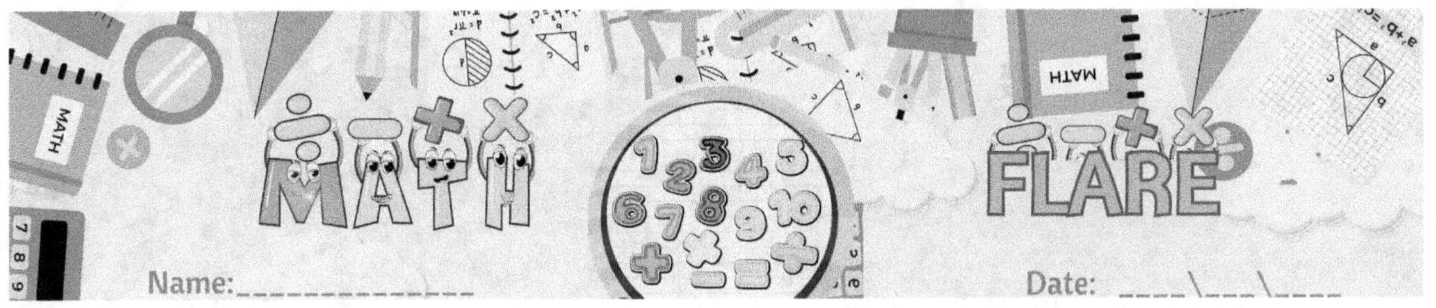

267. $11 - y = 8$

268. $19m - 5 = 14$

269. $9k + 9 = 126$

270. $y + 14 = 20$

271. $6 - 1m = 4$

272. $140 \div y = 14$

273. $119 \div z = 17$

274. $z \times 5 = 20$

275. $24 \div m = 12$

276. $k - 13 = 3$

277. $1 + x = 16$

278. $6 + 16k = 54$

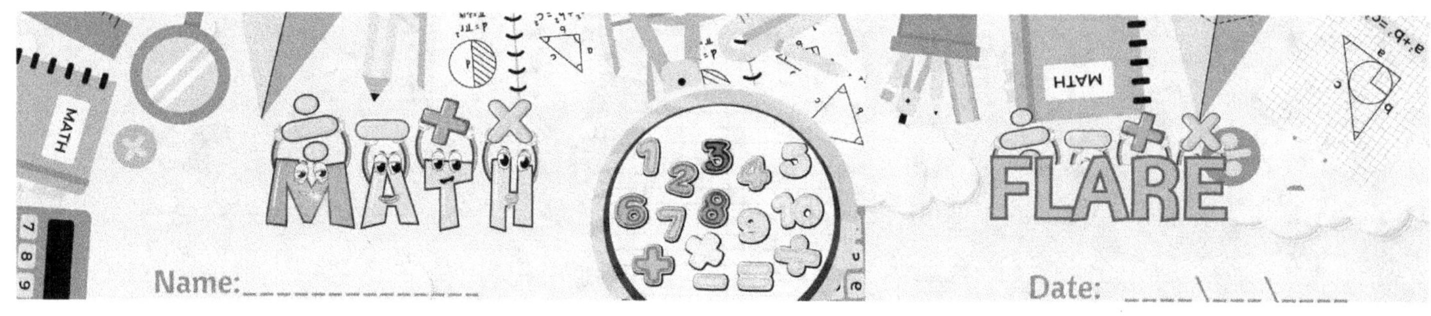

279. $z + 1 = 3$

280. $1x + 18 = 19$

281. $207 - 11y = 9$

282. $y \div 18 = 10$

283. $k - 7 = 7$

284. $13 \times m = 156$

285. $16m - 9 = 215$

286. $11 - m = 2$

287. $m \div 4 = 5$

288. $y \div 12 = 17$

289. $z \times 17 = 204$

290. $k + 14 = 34$

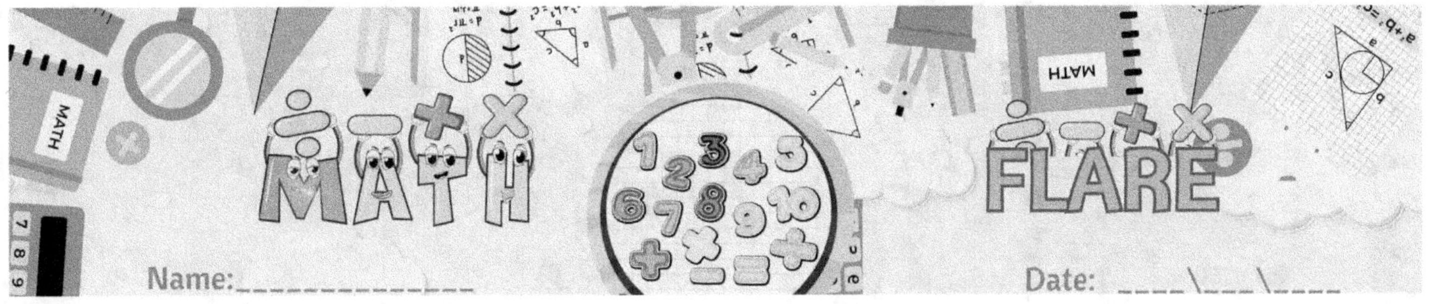

291. $x \div 5 = 11$

292. $m - 6 = 4$

293. $7 - k = 0$

294. $54 \div k = 18$

295. $4 \times z = 44$

296. $y + 3 = 5$

297. $k - 14 = 4$

298. $z \div 15 = 18$

299. $z \times 15 = 120$

300. $265 - 13z = 5$

301. $51 \div y = 3$

302. $z + 16 = 23$

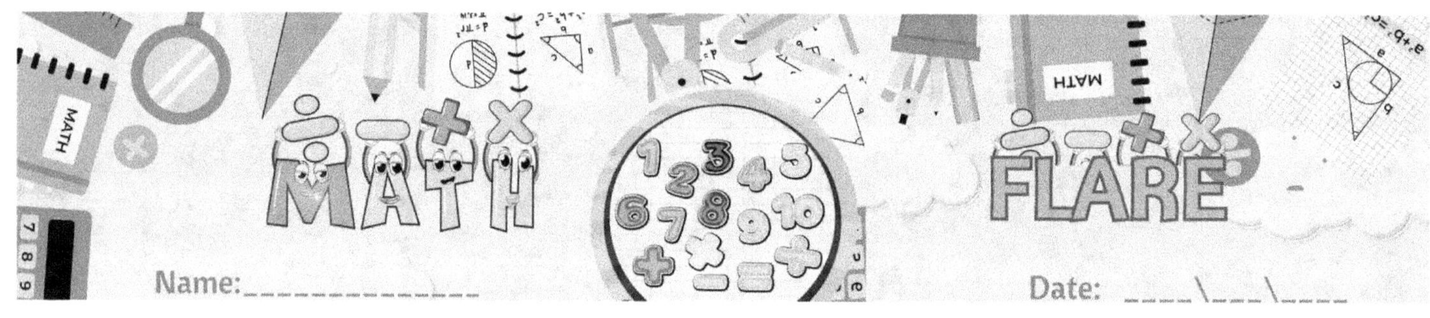

303. $45 \div m = 3$

304. $7y + 14 = 126$

305. $306 \div z = 18$

306. $7 + 10z = 177$

307. $15 - y = 11$

308. $42 - 9y = 6$

309. $5 + y = 23$

310. $z - 1 = 3$

311. $k - 20 = 0$

312. $y \div 8 = 3$

313. $10 - z = 3$

314. $18x + 5 = 113$

315. $14 \times k = 112$

316. $16 + 16k = 160$

317. $17 - m = 9$

318. $11 - z = 5$

319. $2 \times y = 12$

320. $24 \div z = 2$

321. $x - 7 = 5$

322. $14k - 20 = 50$

323. $13 - m = 0$

324. $7 + k = 15$

325. $9 \div m = 3$

326. $286 - 19k = 1$

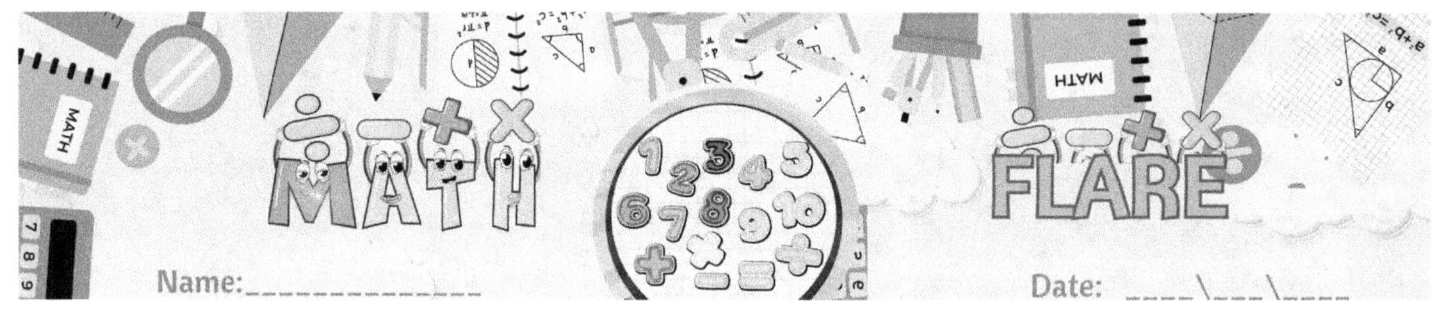

Name:_______________________   Date: _____ \ ____ \ _____

327. 8 + 5x = 48

328. y − 9 = 9

329. 10 ÷ z = 10

330. 19 − y = 6

331. 13 − z = 9

332. y ÷ 1 = 20

333. 28 ÷ m = 7

334. 13 − k = 2

335. 10 + 12z = 190

336. 20y − 12 = 68

337. 16x + 8 = 104

338. 15x − 13 = 122

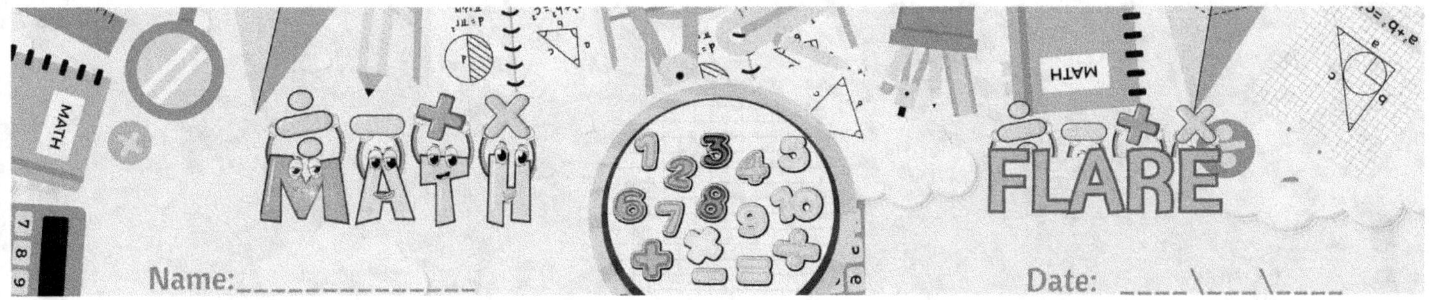

339. $m \times 9 = 54$

340. $m \times 12 = 72$

341. $y + 13 = 21$

342. $7y - 19 = 79$

343. $k - 9 = 7$

344. $16k - 1 = 287$

345. $18 + z = 30$

346. $y - 2 = 15$

347. $12m - 13 = 23$

348. $323 \div x = 19$

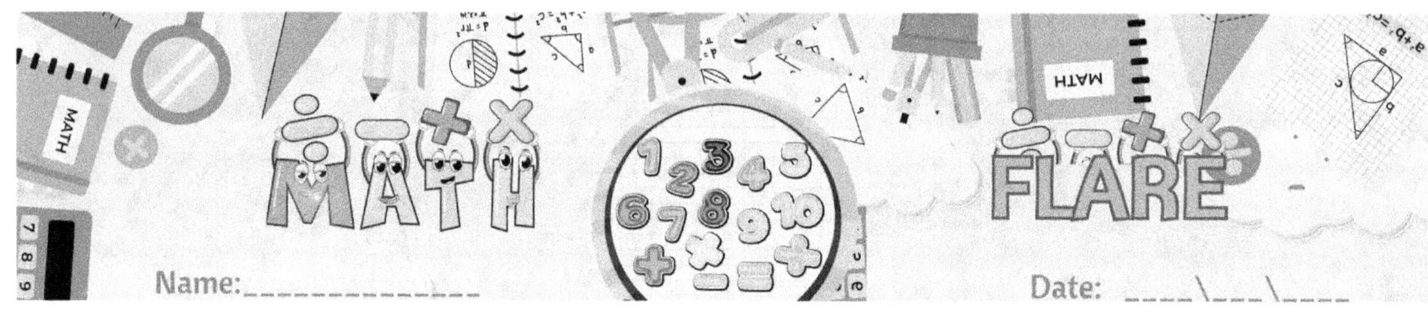

Solving Inequalities

349. $$\frac{m}{-5} \geq -5$$

350. $$-6\,z \geq -10$$

351. $$9 < k + {-4}$$

352. $$3 \leq -2 - m$$

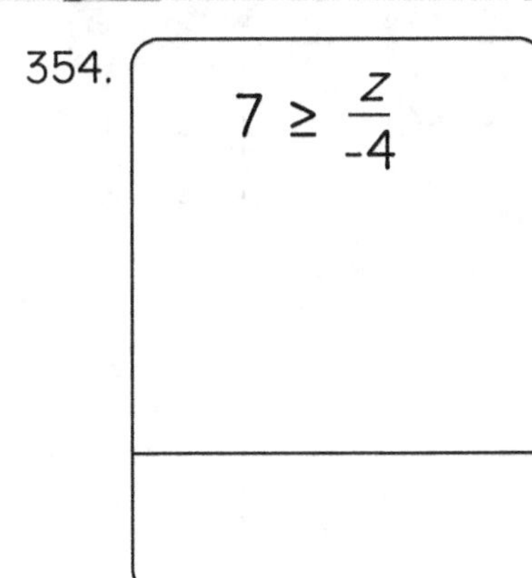

353.

$$9 > 1 - m$$

354.

$$7 \geq \frac{z}{-4}$$

355.

$$z + 1 < 7$$

356.

$$6\,k > -15$$

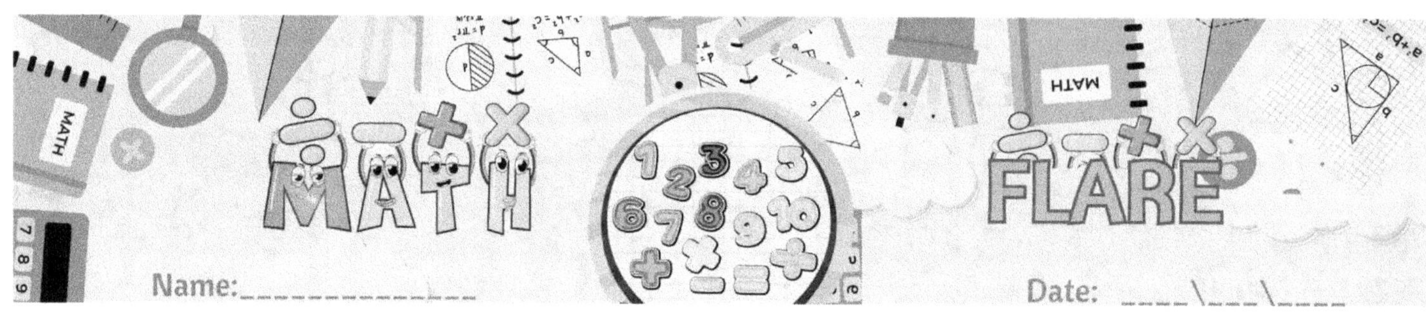

357.

$$\frac{z}{3} \leq -4$$

358.

$$6\,m \leq 18$$

359.

$$3 > -5 - z$$

360.

$$x + 8 \geq -6$$

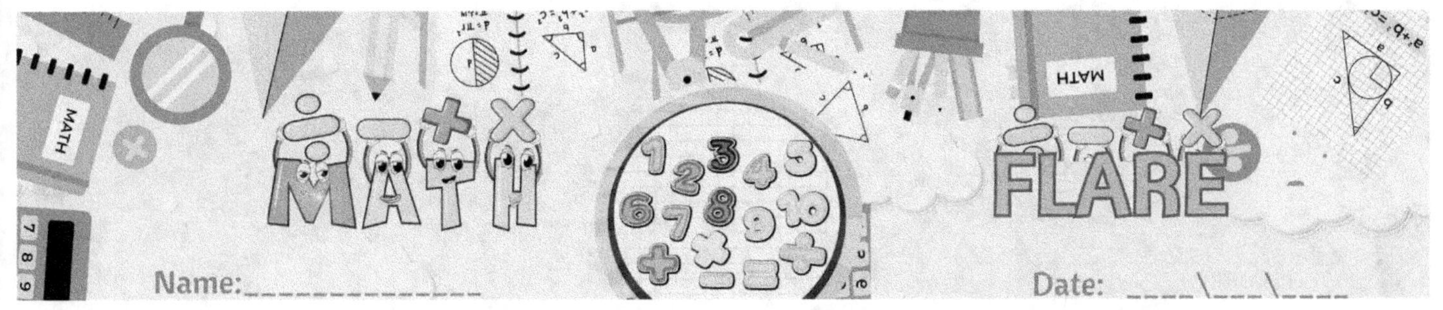

361.

$$-3 \leq k + 2$$

362.

$$18\,m \leq 9$$

363.

$$9 < k - {-8}$$

364.

$$\frac{x}{-3} < -8$$

365.

$-3\,m < 15$

366.

$-3 \leq x + 1$

367. 

$-9 - k > -8$

368. 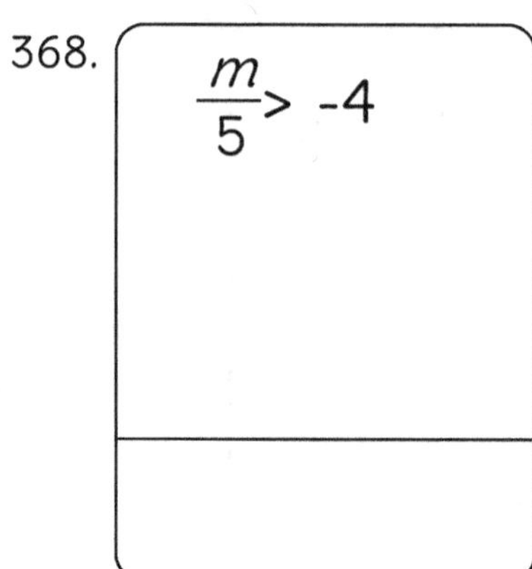

$\dfrac{m}{5} > -4$

369.

$$9 < 7 - z$$

370.

$$-1 + m \leq -6$$

371.

$$1 > \dfrac{z}{-6}$$

372.

$$-6 > -8\,m$$

373.

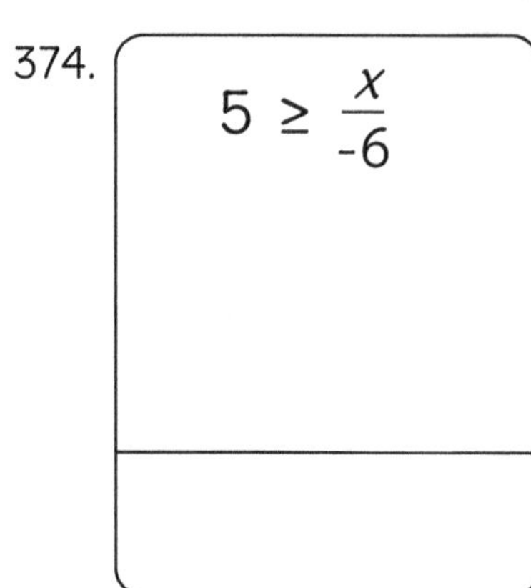

$$6 \geq -2z$$

374.

$$5 \geq \frac{x}{-6}$$

375.

$$-6 > m + -2$$

376.

$$2 \geq 1 - k$$

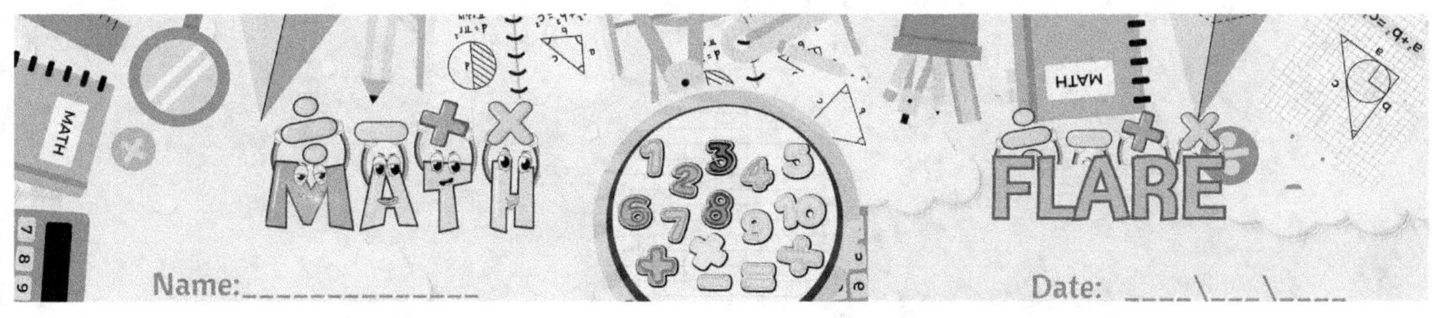

377.

$$\frac{y}{-1} \geq 1$$

378.

$$0 > -5 - x$$

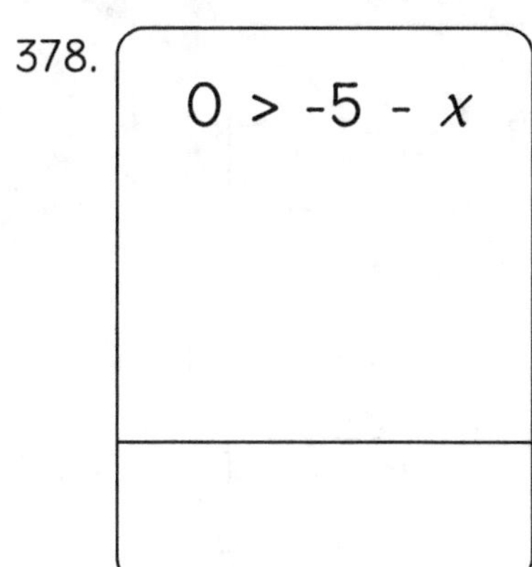

379.

$$9\,x \geq 6$$

380.

$$-7 \geq -4 + y$$

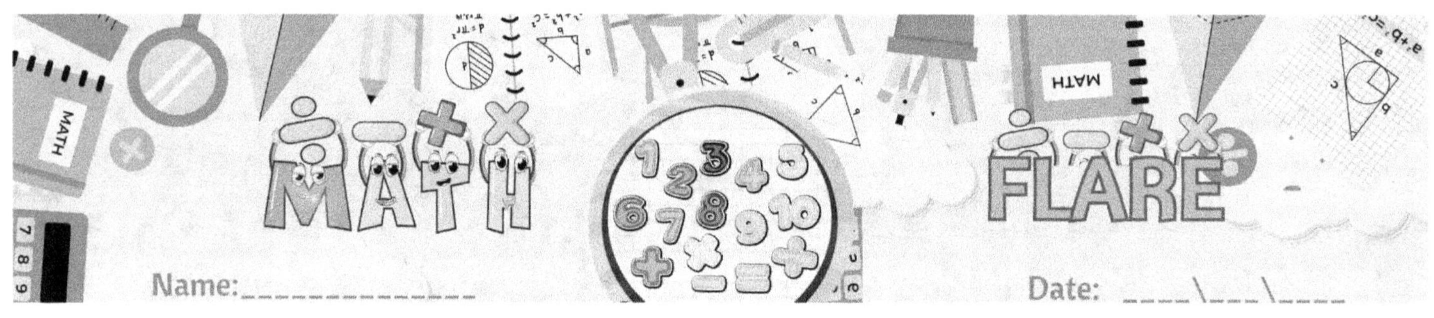

381.
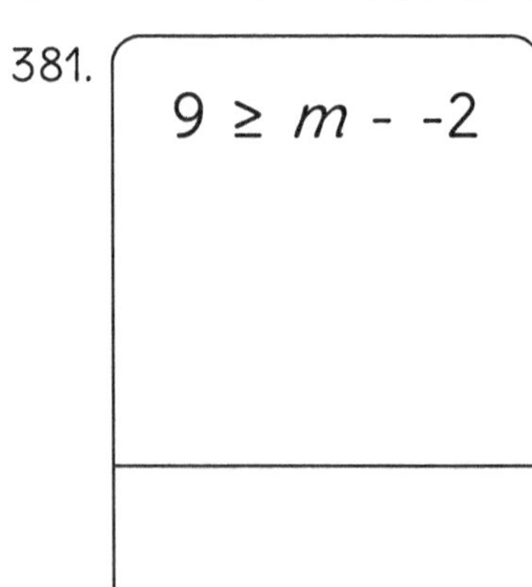

$9 \geq m - -2$

382.

$8 + z < -5$

383.

$-10\ k > 10$

384.

$-9 \geq \dfrac{m}{5}$

385.

$$-10 \geq -12\,y$$

386.

$$\frac{y}{5} > 5$$

387.

$$z - {-4} \geq 9$$

388.

$$-9 < y + {-4}$$

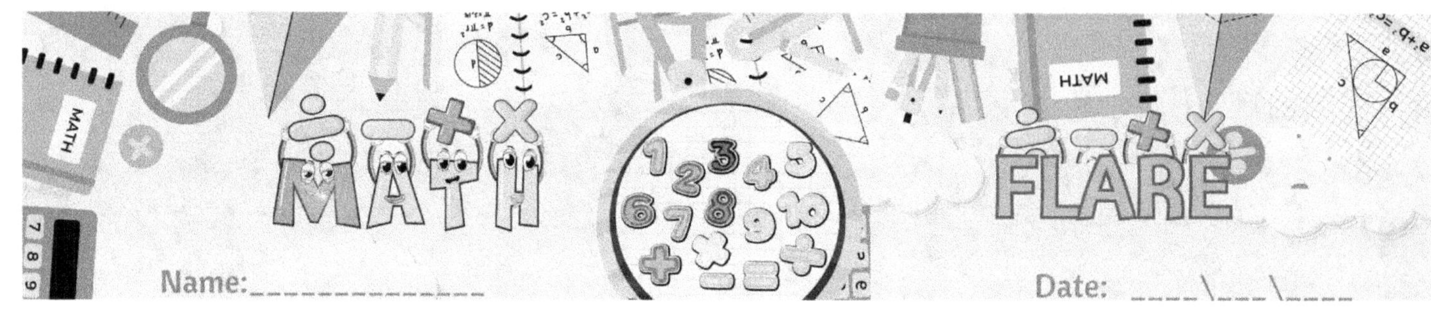

389.

$$-4 < 6 + y$$

390.

$$6x \leq -12$$

391.

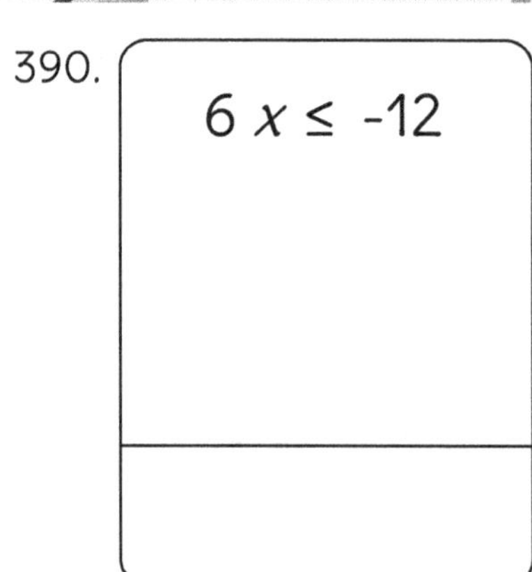

$$\frac{m}{-2} > -7$$

392.

$$9 \leq k - 8$$

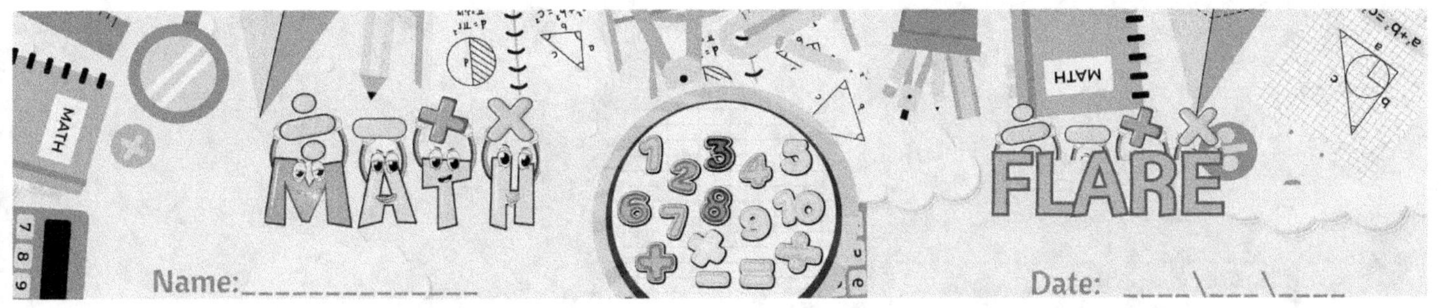

393.

$$-6 \geq 10z$$

394.

$$2 \geq 5 + y$$

395.

$$\frac{x}{-5} \leq -4$$

396.

$$m - {-6} \leq 2$$

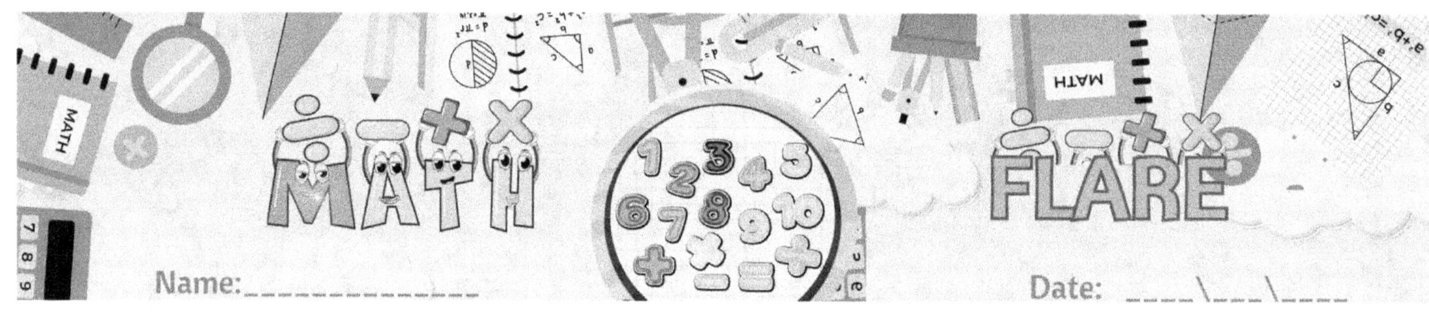

397.
$$-7 \geq z + 7$$

398.
$$6x \leq 2$$

399.
$$\frac{y}{4} > -9$$

400.
$$0 \geq -3 - k$$

401.

$$3 \leq \frac{k}{3}$$

402.

$$-7 + k < -5$$

403.

$$2 \leq y - -2$$

404.

$$-3 < 1z$$

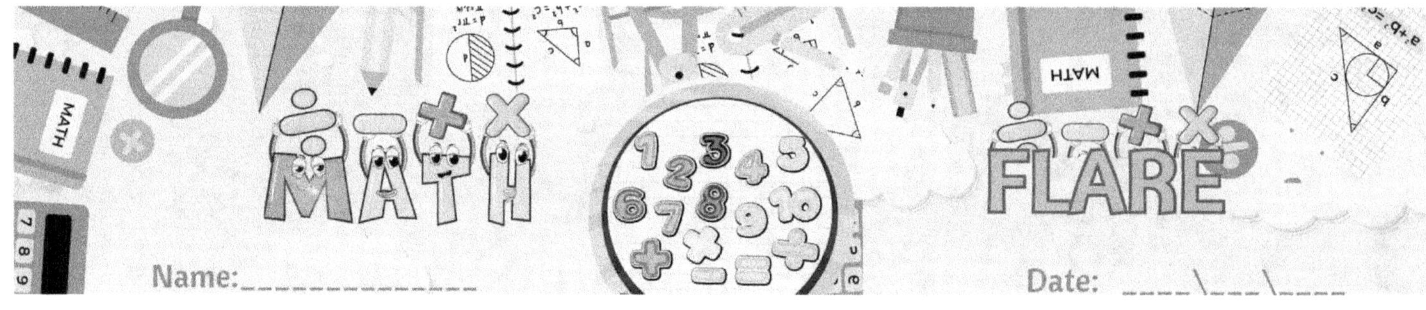

405.

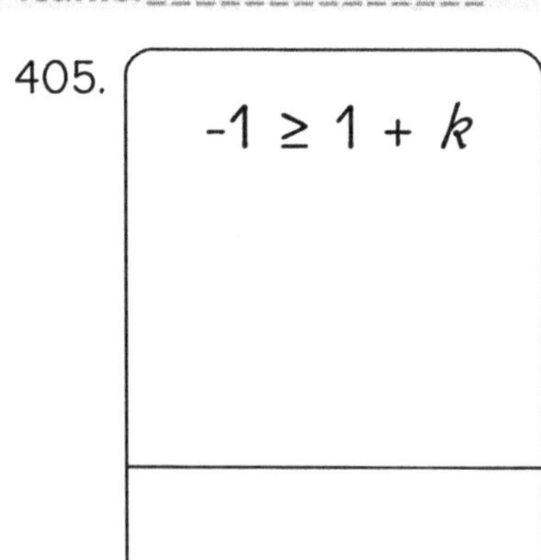

$$-1 \geq 1 + k$$

406.

$$3 - z \leq 5$$

407.

$$18 < -21\,m$$

408.

$$1 \geq \frac{z}{-5}$$

Solving Equations

Evaluate each expression when: x = 6

409. 6 + x =

410. 7 - x =

411. x - 6 =

412. 5 + x =

413. 2 + x =

414. x + 7 =

415. x + 5 =

416. x - 2 =

417. x + 1 =

418. 10 + x =

Solving Equations

Evaluate each expression when: x = 3

419. $x - 1 =$

420. $x + 1 =$

421. $9 - x =$

422. $x - 7 =$

423. $5 + x =$

424. $x - 8 =$

425. $x + 7 =$

426. $x + 2 =$

427. $x - 3 =$

428. $1 - x =$

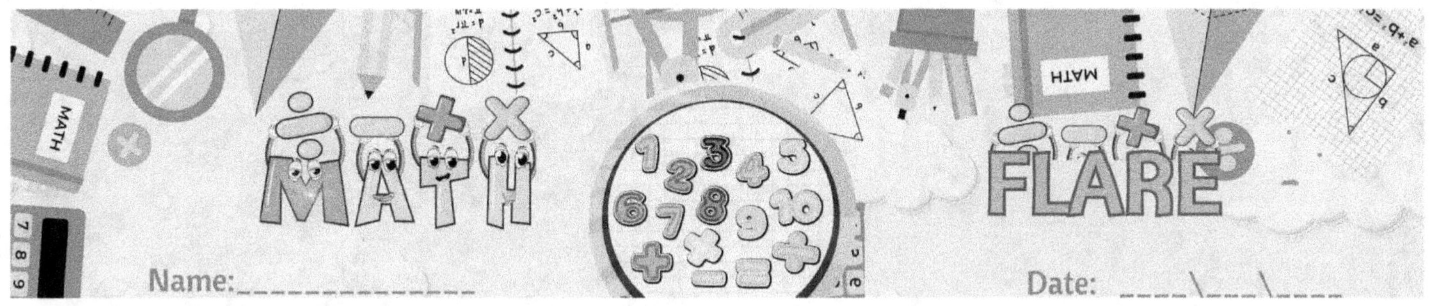

Solving Equations
Evaluate each expression when: x = 6

429. 7 − x =

430. x + 6 =

431. 3 + x =

432. 8 + x =

433. x − 3 =

434. x + 9 =

435. 2 − x =

436. x − 10 =

437. x − 5 =

438. x + 2 =

Solving Equations

Evaluate each expression when: x = 2

439. $4x + 7 =$

440. $10(2 - x) =$

441. $9 + x =$

442. $1 + x =$

443. $4x - x =$

444. $9x - x =$

445. $x - 6 =$

446. $3(4 + x) =$

447. $5x + 4 =$

448. $x + 9 =$

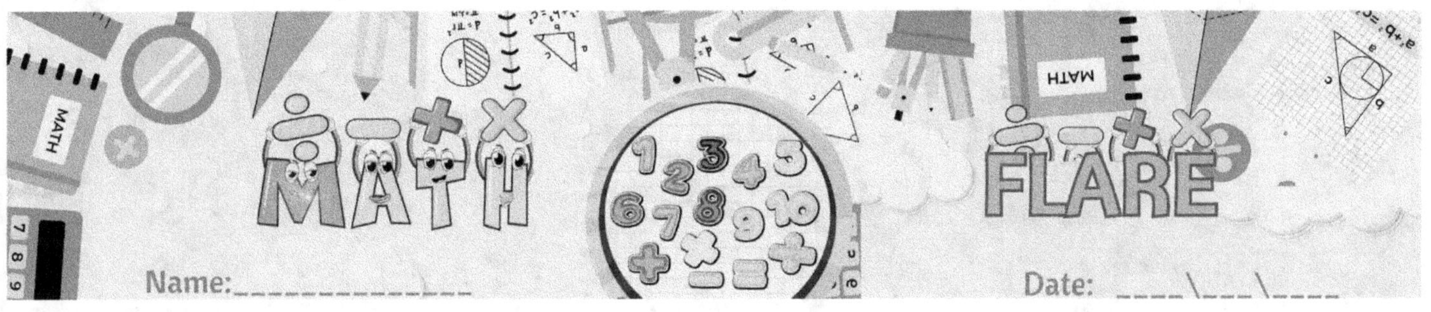

Solving Equations

Evaluate each expression when: x = 1

449. $8(9 - x) =$

450. $4x + x =$

451. $3(7 - x) =$

452. $7 + 8x =$

453. $x - 10 =$

454. $4 - x =$

455. $10x + x - 4 =$

456. $5x + 1 =$

457. $1(6 + x) =$

458. $x + 6 + 4x =$

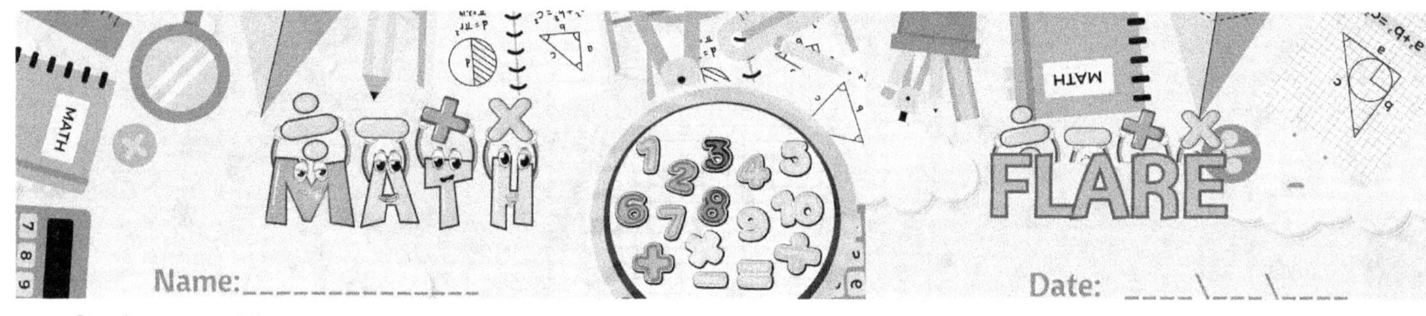

Solving Equations

Evaluate each expression when: x = 3

459. $6x + 4 =$

460. $9 + 10x =$

461. $1 - x =$

462. $x - 2 =$

463. $10(7 - x) =$

464. $9x + 6 =$

465. $x + 7 =$

466. $5x + x =$

467. $x + 9x + 9x =$

468. $9(9 + x) =$

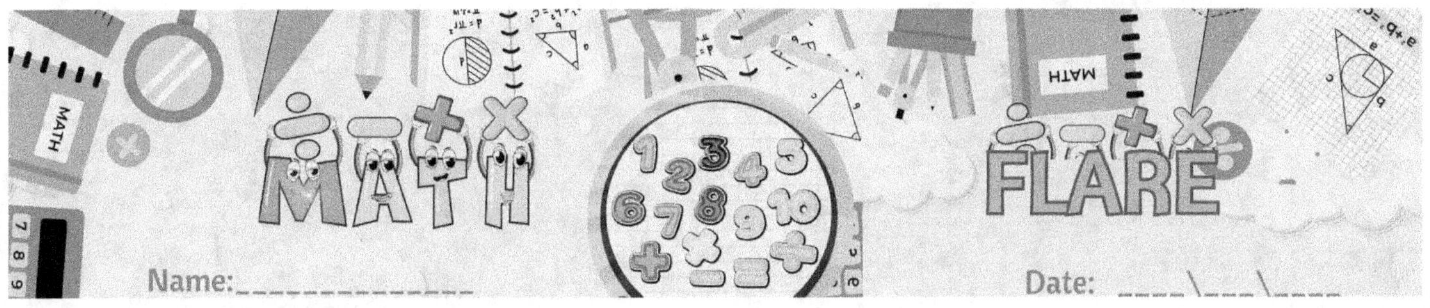

Solving Equations

Evaluate each expression when: $x = 6$

469. $2x - 3 =$

470. $x + 1 + 9x =$

471. $7x + 8 =$

472. $x + 5 =$

473. $x + 2 + 4x =$

474. $3x + 9 =$

475. $10x + x =$

476. $7x + 9 =$

477. $5x + 4 =$

478. $6x + 6 =$

Solving Equations

Evaluate each expression when: x = 7

479. x + 2 =

480. 7x + 8x – 2 =

481. 5x + 7x + 6x =

482. 8x + x =

483. x + 8 + 3x =

484. 4x – x =

485. 7(5 – x) =

486. 5x + 8 =

487. x + 1 =

488. 7x + x =

Solving Equations

Evaluate each expression when: x = 2

489. $7 + x =$

490. $4 - x =$

491. $x + 4 =$

492. $2x + 4 =$

493. $2x - x =$

494. $x + 5 =$

495. $5x + 9 - 9x =$

496. $9 + 8x =$

497. $x + 2 =$

498. $x - 10 =$

Solving Equations

Evaluate each expression when: x = 5

499. $10 + x =$

500. $5 + x =$

501. $1 + x =$

502. $4x - x =$

503. $8 + 9x =$

504. $2(8 - x) =$

505. $3 - x =$

506. $2(4 - x) =$

507. $5x + 10 =$

508. $7 + 6x =$

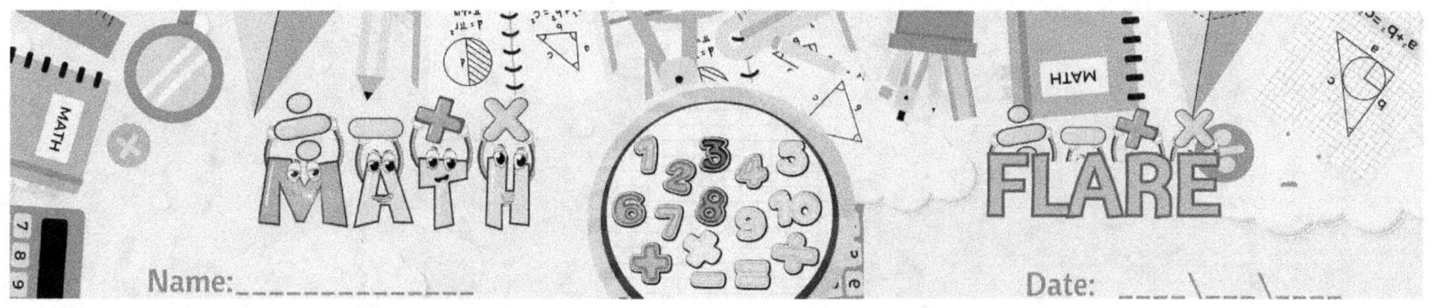

Solving Equations

Evaluate each expression when: $x = 1$

509. $7(7 - x) =$

510. $9x - 2 =$

511. $6(4 + x) =$

512. $7x + 2x + 6x =$

513. $1(9 - x) =$

514. $4x + 1 =$

515. $9(10 + x) =$

516. $x + 5 =$

517. $x + 7 + 7x =$

518. $7x + 6 =$

ANSWERS

Page 1: Order of Operations (PEMDAS)

1. 68	2. 104	3. 53	4. 54	5. 19	6. 64
7. 35	8. 22	9. 144	10. 36	11. 16	12. 33
13. 80	14. 107	15. 104	16. 233	17. 140	18. 96
19. 1.7	20. 36	21. 8	22. 112	23. 218	24. 6
25. 3.8	26. 31	27. 4,905	28. 81	29. 209	30. 26
31. 170	32. 168	33. 32	34. 168	35. 39	36. 66
37. 96	38. 125	39. 1.3	40. 15	41. 225	42. 95
43. 5	44. 132	45. 14	46. 48	47. 90	48. 121
49. 35	50. 17	51. 4	52. 187	53. 16	54. 99
55. 12	56. 53	57. 19	58. 71	59. 68	60. 120
61. -5	62. 20	63. 16	64. 2	65. 1,767	66. 26
67. 156	68. 2.3	69. 116	70. 121	71. 269	72. 96
73. 7	74. 5,191	75. 7	76. 15	77. 2,305	78. 60
79. 45	80. 102	81. 20	82. 9	83. 52	84. 112
85. 93	86. 585	87. 130	88. 60	89. 52	90. 58
91. 36	92. -6	93. 25	94. 23	95. 21	96. 90
97. 1.3	98. 80	99. 24	100. 2	101. 785	102. 17
103. 72	104. 157	105. 57	106. 74	107. 2	108. 30
109. 60	110. 18	111. 1,301	112. 3,142	113. 17	114. 136

115. 17   116. 86   117. 244   118. 24   119. 70   120. 21

121. 13   122. 353   123. 24   124. 3   125. 22   126. 140

127. 14   128. 5   129. 89   130. 70   131. 306   132. 1,771

133. 262   134. 909   135. 9   136. 12   137. 91   138. 100

139. 24   140. 105   141. 14   142. 6   143. 15   144. 22

145. 0   146. 185   147. 117   148. 26

Page 16:   Equations (One Side)

149. $m = 18$ 150. $y = 2$ 151. $m = 2$ 152. $k = 19$ 153. $k = 9$

154. $x = 36$ 155. $m = 17$ 156. $z = 8$ 157. $x = 380$ 158. $x = 12$

159. $x = 15$ 160. $y = 1$ 161. $z = 10$ 162. $k = 14$ 163. $k = 114$

164. $m = 20$ 165. $y = 2$ 166. $y = 7$ 167. $z = 17$ 168. $x = 6$

169. $x = 3$ 170. $y = 6$ 171. $k = 7$ 172. $m = 12$ 173. $z = 8$

174. $m = 17$ 175. $z = 14$ 176. $k = 8$ 177. $k = 14$ 178. $k = 16$

179. $x = 10$ 180. $y = 40$ 181. $y = 13$ 182. $x = 6$ 183. $y = 9$

184. $x = 9$ 185. $y = 13$ 186. $k = 13$ 187. $k = 11$ 188. $x = 17$

189. $m = 16$ 190. $y = 4$ 191. $z = 4$ 192. $m = 4$ 193. $k = 4$

194. $x = 18$ 195. $y = 20$ 196. $k = 8$ 197. $m = 19$ 198. $k = 5$

199. $m = 5$ 200. $x = 8$ 201. $k = 4$ 202. $m = 17$ 203. $x = 3$

204. $y = 16$ 205. $x = 5$ 206. $z = 8$ 207. $k = 5$ 208. $y = 10$

209. $y = 15$ 210. $k = 3$ 211. $z = 17$ 212. $x = 20$ 213. $k = 30$

214. $z = 99$ 215. $k = 10$ 216. $m = 3$ 217. $x = 4$ 218. $y = 11$

219. x = 16   220. x = 15   221. x = 10   222. m = 13   223. m = 16

224. y = 12   225. z = 5   226. z = 12   227. k = 20   228. x = 18

229. x = 6   230. y = 12   231. z = 170   232. z = 11   233. y = 6

234. z = 19   235. y = 34   236. m = 11   237. k = 1   238. z = 3

239. z = 8   240. y = 8   241. k = 260   242. m = 12   243. z = 20

244. k = 15   245. z = 10   246. m = 13   247. k = 20   248. m = 11

249. m = 3   250. m = 17   251. x = 3   252. x = 9   253. x = 19

254. z = 8   255. z = 7   256. y = 19   257. z = 10   258. y = 15

259. z = 198   260. y = 15   261. z = 9   262. x = 18   263. m = 18

264. z = 10   265. m = 16   266. z = 15   267. y = 3   268. m = 1

269. k = 13   270. y = 6   271. m = 2   272. y = 10   273. z = 7

274. z = 4   275. m = 2   276. k = 16   277. x = 15   278. k = 3

279. z = 2   280. x = 1   281. y = 18   282. y = 180   283. k = 14

284. m = 12   285. m = 14   286. m = 9   287. m = 20   288. y = 204

289. z = 12   290. k = 20   291. x = 55   292. m = 10   293. k = 7

294. k = 3   295. z = 11   296. y = 2   297. k = 18   298. z = 270

299. z = 8   300. z = 20   301. y = 17   302. z = 7   303. m = 15

304. y = 16   305. z = 17   306. z = 17   307. y = 4   308. y = 4

309. y = 18   310. z = 4   311. k = 20   312. y = 24   313. z = 7

314. x = 6   315. k = 8   316. k = 9   317. m = 8   318. z = 6

319. y = 6   320. z = 12   321. x = 12   322. k = 5   323. m = 13

324. k = 8   325. m = 3   326. k = 15   327. x = 8   328. y = 18

329. z = 1   330. y = 13   331. z = 4   332. y = 20   333. m = 4

334. k = 11   335. z = 15   336. y = 4   337. x = 6   338. x = 9

339. m = 6   340. m = 6   341. y = 8   342. y = 14   343. k = 16

344. k = 18   345. z = 12   346. y = 17   347. m = 3   348. x = 17

Page 33: Solving Inequalities

349. $m \le 25$ 350. $z \le 5/3$ 351. $k > 13$ 352. $m \le -5$

353. $m > -8$ 354. $z \ge -28$ 355. $z < 6$ 356. $k > -5/2$

357. $z \le -12$ 358. $m \le 3$ 359. $z > -8$ 360. $x \ge -14$

361. $k \ge -5$ 362. $m \le 1/2$ 363. $k > 1$ 364. $x > 24$

365. $m > -5$ 366. $x \ge -4$ 367. $k < -1$ 368. $m > -20$

369. $z < -2$ 370. $m \le -5$ 371. $z > -6$ 372. $m > 3/4$

373. $z \ge -3$ 374. $x \ge -30$ 375. $m < -4$ 376. $k \ge -1$

377. $y \le -1$ 378. $x > -5$ 379. $x \ge 2/3$ 380. $y \le -3$

381. $m \le 7$ 382. $z < -13$ 383. $k < -1$ 384. $m \le -45$

385. $y \ge 5/6$ 386. $y > 25$ 387. $z \ge 5$ 388. $y > -5$

389. $y > -10$ 390. $x \le -2$ 391. $m < 14$ 392. $k \ge 17$

393. $z \le -3/5$ 394. $y \le -3$ 395. $x \ge 20$ 396. $m \le -4$

397. $z \le -14$ 398. $x \le 1/3$ 399. $y > -36$ 400. $k \ge -3$

401. $k \ge 9$ 402. $k < 2$ 403. $y \ge 0$ 404. $z > -3$

405. $k \le -2$ 406. $z \ge -2$ 407. $m < -6/7$ 408. $z \ge -5$

Page 48: Solving Equations

409. 12   410. 1   411. 0   412. 11   413. 8   414. 13   415. 11   416. 4

417. 7   418. 16

Page 49: Solving Equations

419. 2   420. 4   421. 6   422. -4   423. 8   424. -5   425. 10   426. 5

427. 0   428. -2

Page 50: Solving Equations

429. 1   430. 12   431. 9   432. 14   433. 3   434. 15   435. -4   436. -4

437. 1   438. 8

Page 51: Solving Equations

439. 15   440. 0   441. 11   442. 3   443. 6   444. 16   445. -4   446. 18

447. 14   448. 11

Page 52: Solving Equations

449. 64   450. 5   451. 18   452. 15   453. -9   454. 3   455. 7

456. 6   457. 7   458. 11

Page 53: Solving Equations

459. 22   460. 39   461. -2   462. 1   463. 40   464. 33   465. 10

466. 18   467. 57   468. 108

Page 54: Solving Equations

469. 9   470. 61   471. 50   472. 11   473. 32   474. 27   475. 66   476. 51

477. 34   478. 42

Page 55:   Solving Equations

479. 9   480. 103   481. 126   482. 63   483. 36   484. 21

485. -14   486. 43   487. 8   488. 56

Page 56:   Solving Equations

489. 9   490. 2   491. 6   492. 8   493. 2   494. 7   495. 1   496. 25

497. 4   498. -8

Page 57:   Solving Equations

499. 15   500. 10   501. 6   502. 15   503. 53   504. 6   505. -2

506. -2   507. 35   508. 37

Page 58:   Solving Equations

509. 42   510. 7   511. 30   512. 15   513. 8   514. 5   515. 99

516. 6   517. 15   518. 13